CONTENTS

High School Musical 2 Read Along

'What Time Is It?' Sing Along   5

'You Are The Music In Me' Sing Along   6

'I Don't Dance' Sing Along   18

'Bet on It' Sing Along   30

'Everyday' Sing Along   34

Dance Along   38

   41

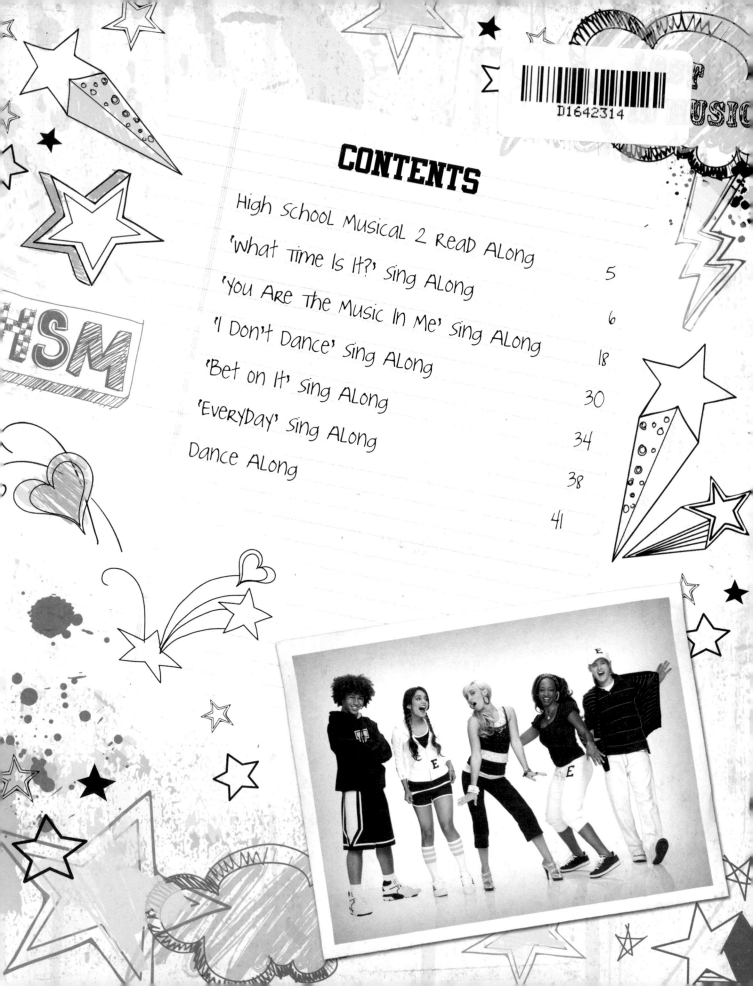

CREDITS

Narrator: Frank Robledano
Troy Bolton: Zac Efron
Gabriella Montez: Vanessa Anne Hudgens
Sharpay Evans: Ashley Tisdale
Ryan Evans: Lucas Grabeel
Chad Danforth: Corbin Bleu
Taylor Mckessie: Monique Coleman
Kelsi Nielsen: Olesya Rulin
Zeke Baylor: Chris Warren Jr
Mr Fulton: Mark L. Taylor
Mr Evans: Robert Curtis Brown
Coach Jack Bolton: Bart Johnson

Engineered by Carlos Vizziello
Read-Along adaptation by Gabriele Bingenheimer

Based on the Disney Channel original Movies
"High School Musical," written by Peter Barsocchini
Based on "High School Musical 2," written by Peter Barsocchini
Based on Characters created by Peter Barsocchini

First published by Parragon in 2008

Parragon
Queen Street House
4 Queen Street
Bath BA1 1HE, UK

ISBN 978-1-4075-3036-9

Printed in China

Songs:

What Time Is It (03:18)
Performed by High School Musical 2 Cast
Written by Matthew Gerrard and Robbie Nevil
© 2007 Walt Disney Music Company (ASCAP)
Produced, Arranged and Mixed by Matthew Gerrard
Keyboards, Guitar, Bass and Programming: Matthew Gerrard
Drums and Percussion: Greg Critchley
Keyboards: Marco Luciani
Additional keyboards: Robbie Nevil
Background Vocals: Robbie Nevil and Lauren Evans

You Are the Music in Me (03:27)
Performed by Troy and Gabriella
Written, Produced and Arranged by Jamie Houston for Goober Boy Productions, Inc.
© 2007 Walt Disney Music Company (ASCAP)
Programming: Jamie Houston and Iki Levy
Engineered by Jamie Houston
Additional Engineering: Dan Rudin
Mixed by Joel Soyffer at Coney Island Studios

I Don't Dance (03:37)
Performed by Chad and Ryan
Written by Matthew Gerrard and Robbie Nevil
© 2007 Walt Disney Music Company (ASCAP)
Produced, Arranged and Mixed by Matthew Gerrard
Keyboards and Programming: Matthew Gerrard and Robbie Nevil
Background Vocals: Robbie Nevil and Lauren Evans

Bet on It (03:18)
Performed by Troy
Written by Antonina Armato and Tim James
© 2007 Walt Disney Music Company (ASCAP)
Produced by Antonina Armato and Tim James
Mixed by Tim James and Paul Palmer

Everyday (04:38)
Performed by Troy and Gabriella
Written, Produced and Arranged by Jamie Houston for Goober Boy Productions, Inc.
© 2007 Walt Disney Music Company (ASCAP)
Programming: Jamie Houston and Iki Levy
Engineered by Jamie Houston
Additional Engineering: Dan Rudin
Mixed by Joel Soyffer at Coney Island Studios

© Disney
(P) 2008 Walt Disney Records

THE *countdown* IS ON!

The **WILDCATS** have just one more training session before our trainer packs his whistle away and the summer break starts at last!

No worries, **TROY** and *Gabriella* will also stay together during the holidays.

But why is *Sharpay* grinning with such confidence?

I've seen that before, she's up to no good!

What *time* is it?

CHORUS

Chad: What time is it
Group: Summertime. It's our vacation.
Chad: What time is it
Group: Party time! That's right, say it LOUD!
Chad: What time is it
Group: The time of our lives, anticipation
Chad: What time is it
Group: Summertime, school's out scream and shout!

Troy: Finally summer's here good to be chillin' out
I'm off the clock, the pressure's off
Now my girl's what it's all about

Gabriella: Ready for some sunshine
For my heart to take a chance
I'm here to stay, not movin' away
Ready for a summer romance
Both: Everybody ready, goin' crazy, yeah we're out
C'mon let me hear you say it now, right now

Chorus

Sharpay: Goodbye to rules, no summer school
I'm free to shop till I drop
It's an education vacation
Ryan: And the party never has to stop
Both: We've got things to do, we'll see ya soon
Sharpay: And we're really gonna miss you all
Ryan: Goodbye to you and you
Sharpay: And you and you
Ryan: Bye-bye until next fall ...b-bye
Both: Everybody ready, goin' crazy, yeah we're out
C'mon let me hear you say it now, right now

Chorus

Troy & Gabriella: No more wakin' up at 6:00a.m
'Cause now our time is all our own

Sharpay & Ryan: Enough already, we're waiting,

Troy, Gabriella,
Chad & Taylor: c'mon Let's go!!! Go outta control!

Troy: Alright

Chad: Everybody

Ryan: Yeah

Troy: C'mon

CHANT

Chad & Group: School Pride let's show it
We're champions and we know it
Wildcats, (yeah) are the best (yeah)
Red, white and gold
When it's time to win we do it
We're number one, we proved it
So let's live it up (yeah), party down

Everybody: That's what this summer's all about

Gabriella: What time is it

Everybody: Summertime is finally here

Troy & Gabriella: Let's celebrate

Everybody: Wanna hear you loud and clear now

Chad & Taylor: School's out

Everybody: We can sleep as late as we want to

Sharpay & Ryan: It's our time

Chad: Now we can do whatever we wanna do

Group: What time is it

It's summertime

We'll be lovin' it

Chad: C'mon and say it again now

Group: What time is it

It's party time

Let's go and have the time of our lives

yeah

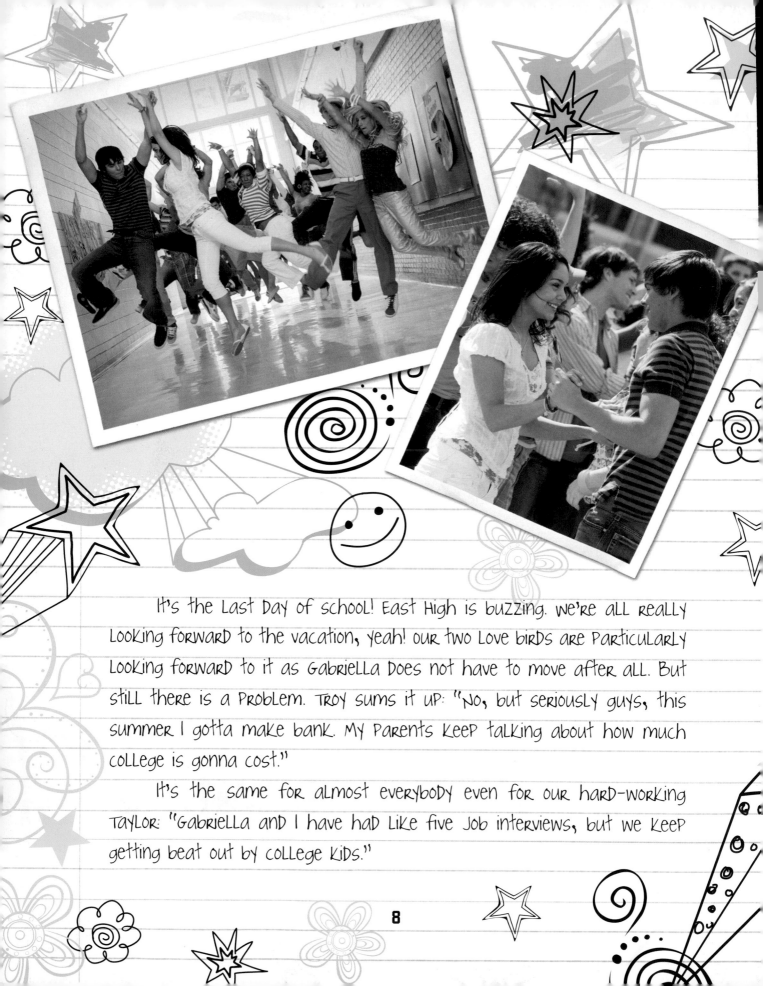

It's the Last Day of School! East High is buzzing. We're all really looking forward to the vacation, yeah! Our two Love birds are Particularly looking forward to it as Gabriella does not have to move after all. But still there is a Problem. Troy sums it up: "No, but seriously guys, this summer I gotta make bank. My Parents keep talking about how much college is gonna cost."

It's the same for almost everybody even for our hard-working Taylor: "Gabriella and I have had like five job interviews, but we keep getting beat out by college kids."

Gabriella is standing alone at her locker. She's quite frustrated because she hasn't found a vacation job yet. So TROY goes over to comfort her: "Hey, whatever happens, as long as we're together it's cool, right?"

"You promise?"

"Here's my promise." And he puts a chain around her neck with a "T"-initial pendant.

Gabriella beams: "T as in TROY?" Of course. This would be the ideal opportunity to steal a kiss, but CHAD, TAYLOR and a few of the gang are coming around the corner. Bad timing ...

9

Ryan and Sharpay don't have to worry about jobs, they have rich parents. But still they watch with some envy as we leave the school totally excited. You can't buy everything with money, right? Sharpay thinks differently: "Ryan, who's the absolute primo boy at East High?"

"I'd say, Troy Bolton has that category pretty much locked up, don't you think?" Yes. And, because Troy is the basketball star and the school super guy, Sharpay wants him to be her boyfriend. Ryan doesn't know how his sister is going to oust Gabriella, but this blonde is not dumb.

She has a plan: "It's summer, Ry. Everything changes."

After school, Ryan and Sharpay Evans drive to a posh and unbelievably expensive golf course where they are expected. "Welcome back to Lava Springs."

"Thank you, Charles. It's good to be home. Oh, can you find some shade for my car?"

The manager, Thomas Fulton, takes care of it himself: "Even if we have to plant a tree."

Mr Fulton doesn't need to do any gardening; he is given a special task. He discreetly calls Troy Bolton: "This is Thomas Fulton, General Manager of Lava Springs Country Club here in Albuquerque. I understand you've been looking for summer work." At first, Troy thinks he didn't hear that right because we are making quite a lot of noise. But Mr Fulton is actually offering him a job.

Troy is excited: "That sounds fantastic, Mr Fulton. But how'd you get my name?" Mr Fulton skillfully avoids answering this question ...

Dive In

Sharpay can be pleased now. Everything is going to plan, as are the preparations for the Midsummer Night Talent Show that is staged each year at the golf club. No need to guess who is going to win this year because Sharpay and Ryan pick up the Star Dazzle Award every year. But our little supermodel wants more, she wants Troy!

And right on time here comes our basketball star Sharpay jumps up, smiles and freezes. From behind Troy the Wildcats and Gabriella appears. Sharpay is shocked! She stumbles and splashes into the pool. Seeing Sharpay struggle, Gabriella jumps in and rescues her. "I've got you."

"What are you doing here?"

Gabriella smiles, "I'm the new lifeguard."

Sharpay storms up to the manager in a rage: "I told you to hire Troy Bolton, not the entire East High student body!"

"You told me to hire Troy Bolton whatever it takes."

And, Troy is the captain of the Wildcats after all. Of course, he is going to negotiate jobs for his friends. Sharpay wasn't banking on that: "Well, why didn't you warn me about the rest of them?"

The manager has a simple explanation for this: "I did discuss the matter with the Lava Springs board, of course."

The board is Mrs. Evans, Sharpay's mother, and she thinks it is good that we are breathing new life into the club. So our little blonde needs to change tactics. "Fulton, if you can't fire them, make them wanna quit." That applies above all to Gabriella Montez ...

We Wildcats don't know anything about Sharpay's schemes. We're just happy to have jobs. Mr. Fulton assigns most of us to kitchen jobs, Troy and Chad are waiters. The curly haired one immediately spots a problem: "Mr. Fulton, your excellency, sir, would it be okay if we draw straws to see who has to wait on Sharpay?"

"Please, none of you will be waiting on Sharpay. You will be serving 'Miss Evans'."

Gabriella bursts into the kitchen. It's her lunch break, but she is three minutes too early. For Mr. Fulton, that's enough for a reprimand: "Three infractions of any kind and your employment is terminated."

Phew, work is over for today. Troy and Gabriella are having a picnic on the golf course. That is, of course, against the rules, but Troy isn't really bothered as he is concerned about something else: "I always liked the idea of being in charge of my future. Until it actually started happening."

Yeah, most of us are worried about what the future will bring. But Gabriella takes it more relaxed: "So, let's just think about right now, because I've never been in one place for an entire summer and this means a lot to me."

Sharpay is secretly watching the couple and takes action. She turns the sprinklers on, but that doesn't bother the love birds at all. They dance under the fountains of water without a care. So Sharpay sends the manager: "First a break time infraction. Now frolicking on the golf course. We are not off to an auspicious start, are we, Miss Montez?"

Next day, Kelsi, our little composer, has a surprise for us: "I am so excited about the club's talent show. I mean, the employees get to do a number, and I have ideas for everyone."

TROY knows what that means: "Big timeout on that one. My singing career began and ended with the East High winter musical." But our captain cannot get out of it that easily. It would be a real pity if he and Gabriella didn't sing together, right? So we talk him round and win him over especially when he hears Kelsi's latest song!

You are the
music in me

Kelsi:

Na, na, na, na
Na, na, na, na, yeah
You are the music in me

You know the words "once upon a time"
Make you listen, there's a reason

Kelsi and Gabriella:

When you dream there's a chance you'll find
A little laughter, or happy ever after

Gabriella and Troy:

You're a harmony to the melody
That's echoing inside my head
A single voice above the noise
And like a common thread
You're pulling me

CHORUS

When I hear my favourite song
I know that we belong
You are the music in me
It's living in all of us
It's brought us here because
You are the music in me

Na, na, na, na
Na, na, na, na, yeah
You are the music in me

TROY AND
GABRIELLA:

It's like I knew you before we met
Can't explain it, there's no name for it
I sang you words I've never said
And it was easy
Because you see the real me
As I am, you understand
And that's more than I've ever known
To hear your voice above the noise
And know I'm not alone
oh, you're singing to me

Chorus

Together we're gonna sing
We got the power to say what we feel
Connected and real
Can't keep it all inside

Na, na, na, na
Na, na, na, na, yeah
You are the music in me (repeat)

Chorus

Na, na, na, na
Na, na, na, na, yeah
Na, na, na, na
You are the music in me

Ryan hears Kelsi's song too and immediately tells his sister: "It's an amazing song, but Kelsi didn't write it for us." Sharpay stays remarkably calm:

"Ryan, it might be wonderful if Troy participates in our talent show." Of course, she already has a plan, but it does not include Gabriella: "I'm not certain Gabriella is ideally suited to help Troy realize his full potential at Lava Springs."

Next morning, Mr. Fulton comes into the kitchen and grabs Troy and Chad: "Danforth, Bolton. You're caddying today. Forty dollars a bag. You've been requested."

"What?" Troy wants to know more, but Chad just says:

"Dude, who cares? For forty bucks I'd caddy for Godzilla."

"Close, very close." Fulton's answer should have actually warned the boys ...

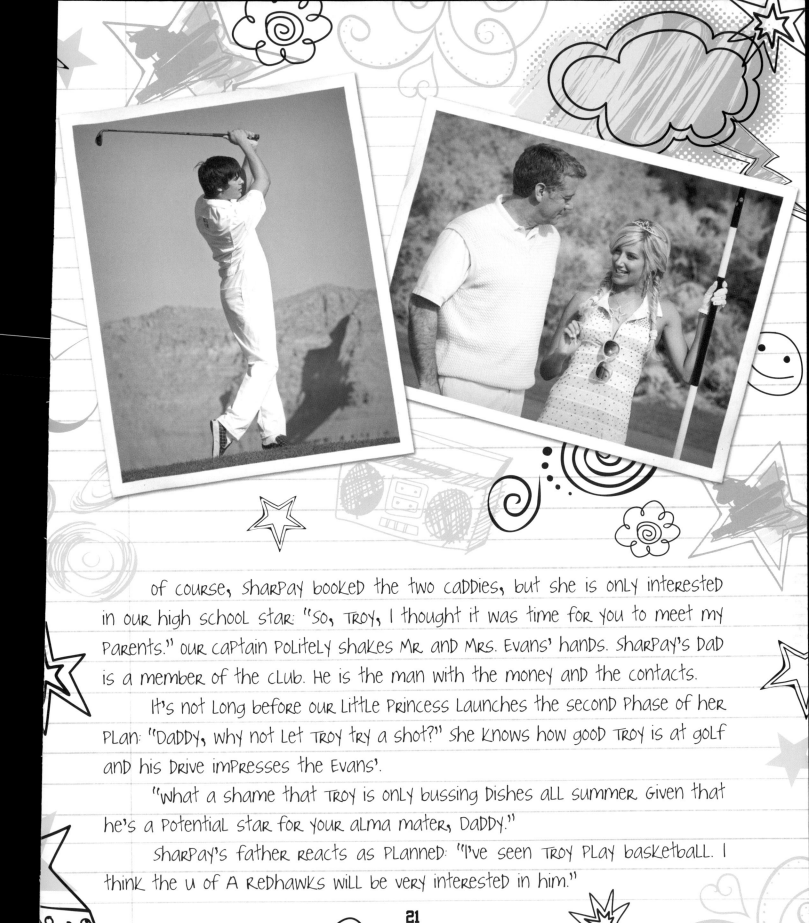

of course, Sharpay booked the two caddies, but she is only interested in our high school star: "So, Troy, I thought it was time for you to meet my parents." Our captain politely shakes Mr and Mrs. Evans' hands. Sharpay's dad is a member of the club. He is the man with the money and the contacts.

It's not long before our little princess launches the second phase of her plan: "Daddy, why not let Troy try a shot?" She knows how good Troy is at golf and his drive impresses the Evans'.

"What a shame that Troy is only bussing dishes all summer. Given that he's a potential star for your alma mater, Daddy."

Sharpay's father reacts as planned: "I've seen Troy play basketball. I think the U of A Redhawks will be very interested in him."

That evening TROY is relieved of waitering duties! Mr. Fulton hands him a suit and tie. "It goes around your neck. Like a, um, dog collar."

Once TROY has changed, Mr. Fulton pushes him into the dining room where Mr. Evans is waiting: "What do you say we get some food, and we can talk about your future."

Sharpay explains: "Daddy's on the board of directors at the university of Albuquerque." They decide who gets awarded scholarships and TROY desperately needs one to go to college.

That is also why Sharpay's father has invited Peter: "So TROY, I saw your championship game. I mean, wow! That last-second shot at the buzzer .... outstanding."

The Wildcats captain points at Chad and Jason, who are just serving the food: "Actually, my teammates here stole the ball ...."

Troy feels terrible. And, Sharpay has pressed him into singing with her. He tries to get out of it, but Sharpay keeps on at him: "But you will sing some other time with me? Promise?" Everyone at the table is looking at him expectantly.

Troy gives in: "Promise."

At last he can go. He races to the pool where he has a date with Gabriella "Sorry I'm late!" and jumps into the water.

Gab hesitates: "You know we're not supposed to be in the pool." But then she jumps in too. They splash around in the water and Troy moves close to her.

"You know, right now with you, it's finally starting to feel like summer." He goes to kiss her ... oops, Fulton is standing there next to the pool. Gabriella has just got her second warning.

"Don't get a third," he scolds.

When Troy gets home, he tells his father that the Evans' have invited him over for dinner: "And they were talking about scholarships while Jason and Chad were like ... serving me. It felt weird." His father doesn't think anything of it:

"A scholarship's special, that's why there's only a few to go around. Nothing wrong with keeping your eye on the prize." Troy still feels uneasy ...

Next morning, our captain tries to put in a good word for Gabriella: "About the pool thing last night, you can't blame Gabriella."

"I'm promoting you." Mr. Fulton is, as ever, full of surprises. Instead of giving him a warning, he offers Troy an amazing job as a golf instructor for children.

Troy just can't believe it: "That's off the hook! I-I think it sounds very manageable."

It does have a catch though, Mr. Fulton tells him somewhat in passing: "You have complete use of club facilities, but do so prudently. Meaning: fellow Wildcats? Not!"

Troy is standing in front of his new locker: golf clothes, Italian golf shoes and a perfectly equipped golf bag! "How did this happen?"

"It would seem that the Evans family thinks you have untapped potential. And this family has real clout. So I suggest you take the ride."

So Troy is now a golf instructor for kids and for Sharpay! Of course, she takes advantage of that. "By the end of summer, you'll have me playing like a pro."

Her golf club whooshes over Troy: "If I live that long!" She pretends to be so stupid that Troy has to guide her arm. She leans close against him, gives him a longing look and chats about the talent show.

"And here's the best news: All the Redhawk boosters will be there. We'll lock up your scholarship with a high 'C' right from centre stage."

Troy holds out: "Your parents have been really, really nice, Sharpay. But singing with you isn't a part of my job."

"I know. Just something you PROMISED to do. Remember?"

Scheming Sharpay has everything under control, kelsi is next on her List.

"Uh, that new duet that TROY and Gabriella sing? I need it." Our composer fends her off:

"Actually, it's not available." But she doesn't stand a chance against Sharpay.

"You're an employee, not a fairy godmother TROY and I will be doing it in the talent show. oh, and brighten up the tempo." Now it's official. Gabriella is out of the running in the talent show, TROY is going to sing with Sharpay. Her brother is flabbergasted.

"What about our song?"

"Change in plans. I'll find a song for you somewhere in the show. or the next show."

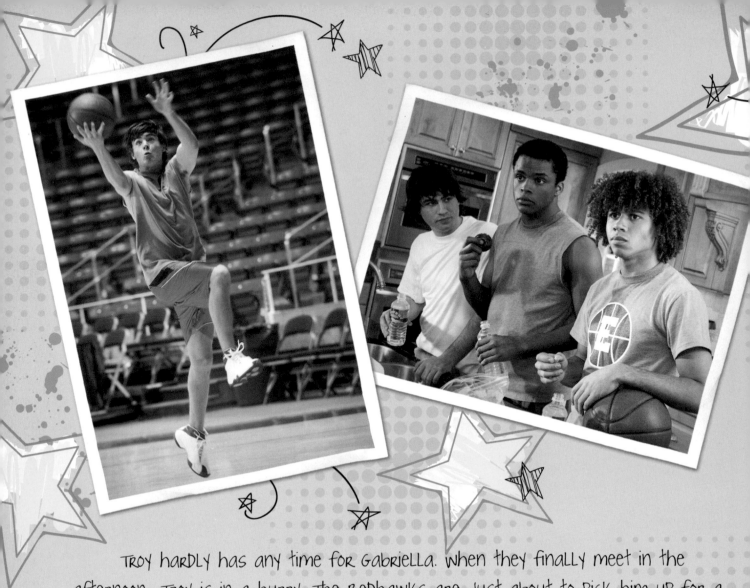

TROY hardly has any time for Gabriella. When they finally meet in the
afternoon, TROY is in a hurry. The REDhawks are just about to pick him up for a
trial. "But I'll be back in about an hour I promise!"

Sadness is written on Gabriella's face. "'Promise' is a really big word, TROY.
And we've got the staff baseball game after work. Remember, you 'promised'
that you'd play." TROY has completely forgotten about the baseball game.

Right now, the REDhawks drop by. And Chad and Zeke do too because TROY
was supposed to be shooting a few hoops with them. Zeke tries to make the best
out of it. "Hey! Why don't you tell them to come over here and mix it up. We'll
show them some game."

"It's a closed practice. Sorry."

Chad glares at TROY. "Maybe you can get us a video?"

When it comes round to the baseball game, everyone has heard that Troy is singing with Sharpay. That means the Wildcats' performance is off. But Gabriella will not give up: "It's our summer, remember? I thought we decided doing the show would be fun."

Jason shrugs his shoulders. "We don't know how to put together a show."

"No. But he does." Gabriella points at Ryan. "If we have a real director putting it together, it could be great."

Chad isn't sure, but Ryan shows him what he can do during the baseball game. And Chad realizes how much baseball and dancing have in common.

I don't dance

Chad and Team: Hey oh Play ball
Chad: ooo ooo ooo
Chad and Team: Hey, hey oh
Ryan and Team: Hey batter batter, hey batter batter, swing
Chad: I've got to just do my thing
Ryan and Team: Hey batter batter, hey batter batter, swing
Ryan: I'll show you that it's one and the same
Baseball, Dancing, same game
It's easy
Step up to the plate, start swingin'
Chad: I wanna play ball now and that's all
This is what I do
It ain't no dance that you can show me
Team: Hey, hey, hey
Chad: Yeah
Girls in
the stands: You'll never know
Chad: oh, I know
Girls in
the stands: If you never try
Chad: There's just one little thing
stops me every time   Yeah
Ryan: C'mon

CHORUS

Chad and Team: I Don't Dance
Ryan, Team
and Girls: I know you can
Chad: Not a chance No
Ryan, Team
and Girls: If I can Do this,
well you can do that

Chad and Team: But I Don't Dance
Ryan and Team: Hit it out of the Park
Chad and Team: I Don't Dance
Ryan, Team
and Girls: I say you can
Chad and Team: There's not a chance
Ryan, Team
and Girls: Slide home, you score,
swingin' on the Dance floor
Chad and Team: I Don't Dance, no
Ryan and Team: Hey batter batter, hey batter batter, sw
Chad: I've got to just do my thing
Ryan and Team: Hey batter batter, hey batter batter, sw
Chad: Yeah, yeah, yeah, yeah
Ryan: Two steppin' now you're up to bat
Bases Loaded, Do your Dance
It's easy
Take your best shot   Just hit it
Chad: I've got what it takes
playin' my game
so you better spin that pitch you're
gonna throw me
I'll show you how I swing
Girls in
the stands: You'll never know
Chad: oh I know
Girls in
the stands: If you never try

30

Chad: There's just one little thing stops me
every time   yeah

Ryan: C'mon

CHORUS

RAP SECTION

Ryan and Team: Lean back, tuck it in, take a chance
Swing it out, spin around, do the Dance

Chad and Team: I wanna play ball not Dance hall
I'm makin' a triple not a curtain call

Ryan and Team: I can prove it to you till you know it's true
'cause I can swing it I can bring it to
the Diamond too

Chad and Team: You're talkin' a lot, show me what you got
Stop

Everybody: Swiiiiing!
SWING SECTION
Team: Hey, swing it like this
Chad: Yeah   oh~
Ryan: Swing
Chad: ooooh
Ryan: Jitterbug
Team: Just like that   oh
Ryan: That's what I mean
That's how you swing
Chad: You make a good pitch
but I Don't believe
Ryan: I say you can
Chad: I know I can't   I Don't
Ryan and Chad: Dance

CHAD STOMP SECTION

Ryan, Team
and Girls: You can do it

Chad: I Don't Dance, no

Ryan, Team
and Girls: Nothin' to it
Atta boy   atta boy   yeah

Chad and Team: Hey batter batter, hey batter batter,
what

Ryan and Team: 1 2 3 4   everybody swing
C'mon
CHORUS

31

It's a deal: Ryan will be director, Kelsi will write a new song and we Wildcats will sing and dance and Chad will dance too! Well, we are actually pretty good. So Sharpay starts to get cold feet and whines to her brother: "Do you want us to lose the Star Dazzle Award to a bunch of ... Dishwashers!"

"Us?" Ryan doesn't have to suck up to Sharpay anymore. He brushes his sister off! So she takes a different route ...

An official order soon comes from Mr. Fulton. Taylor reads: "No staff participation in the show will be allowed. No exceptions."

Kelsi knows that it wasn't Fulton's idea: "Unless Fulton suddenly has blonde hair and wears designer flip-flops."

Gabriella is through. She is furious and storms over to Sharpay. "Forget about the rest of us, how about the fact that your brother has worked extremely hard on the show."

But 'Miss Evans' stays firm: "You don't like the fact that I won."

"What's the prize? Troy? The Star Dazzle Award?" Gabriella does not want to play along with this game. "So I'm done here. But you better step away from the mirror long enough to check the damage that will always be right behind you." Gabriella leaves the club and the 'new' Troy! She hands him back the chain and pendant with tears in her eyes.

Troy is devastated. Gabriella has gone and he has fallen out with Chad. Everything that means anything to him is falling apart. Everything is changing. "I don't even know who I am anymore."

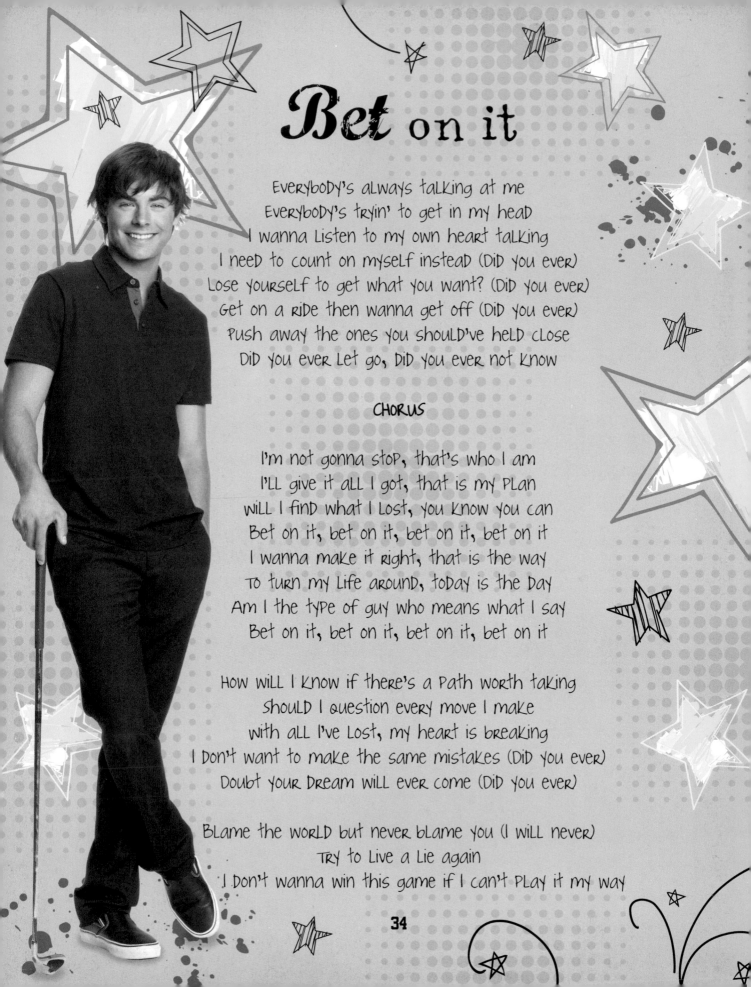

Bet on it

Everybody's always talking at me
Everybody's tryin' to get in my head
I wanna listen to my own heart talking
I need to count on myself instead (Did you ever)
Lose yourself to get what you want? (Did you ever)
Get on a ride then wanna get off (Did you ever)
Push away the ones you should've held close
Did you ever let go, did you ever not know

CHORUS

I'm not gonna stop, that's who I am
I'll give it all I got, that is my plan
Will I find what I lost, you know you can
Bet on it, bet on it, bet on it, bet on it
I wanna make it right, that is the way
To turn my life around, today is the day
Am I the type of guy who means what I say
Bet on it, bet on it, bet on it, bet on it

How will I know if there's a path worth taking
Should I question every move I make
With all I've lost, my heart is breaking
I don't want to make the same mistakes (Did you ever)
Doubt your dream will ever come (Did you ever)

Blame the world but never blame you (I will never)
Try to live a lie again
I don't wanna win this game if I can't play it my way

34

Chorus

Oh, hold up
Do what you think
Bring it on now
Gotta work on my swing
Gotta do my own thing
Oh, hold up

It's no good at all to see yourself
And not recognize your face
Out on my own it's such a scary place
The answers are all inside of me
All I got to do is believe

I'm not gonna stop
Not gonna stop 'til I get my shot
That's who I am, that is my plan
Will I end up on top again
Bet on it, bet on it, bet on it, bet on it
You can bet on it, bet on it, bet on it, bet on it

I wanna make it right, that is the way
To turn my life around, today is the day
Am I the type of guy who means what I say
Bet on it, bet on it, bet on it, bet on it
You can bet on me

Troy now knows what he doesn't want! And Sharpay hits the roof: "What do you mean you're not doing the show?"

"Sharpay, I don't like the way you've been treating my friends. And I don't like the way I've been treating them either. So I'm doing something about it." So now he is a waiter again: "I'm an employee. Employees aren't allowed in the show."

The news spreads like wildfire. At last, we have the 'old' Troy back again. "Guys, I messed up your show and I'm sorry." Of course, we are no longer angry with him and everything is fine with Chad again.

Only Sharpay is getting a raw deal. She doesn't have a singing partner Ryan does not want to perform with her anymore, but he has quite a cool plan. "Troy, listen. I-I don't really want to see my sister crash and burn. I think you should sing with her."

The time has come, the audience is slowly drifting in. Sharpay is sitting in her dressing room crying, then Troy walks in. "How's your show going?"

"My show makes the captain of the Titanic look like he won the lottery."

"I'll sing with you, Sharpay. I do the show if the Wildcats do the show."

Sharpay agrees to this, of course. "I just wish you were doing this for me." When Troy goes back into the kitchen, Ryan has a surprise for him.

"Hey, speaking of my sister, she wants you to learn a new song." With the help of Kelsi, Troy practices up until the time of his performance and then he runs into Sharpay.

"Hey. Why'd you switch songs?" Sharpay doesn't know what he is talking about.

"But I didn't learn a new song."

"Exactly," comments Ryan as he pushes Troy out onto the stage ...

Everyday

TROY: once in a Lifetime means there's no second chance
So I believe that you and me
Should grab it while we can

Gabriella: Make it Last Forever
Never give it back

TROY and Gabriella: It's our turn, and I'm Lovin' where we're at
Because this moment's really all we have

CHORUS

EVERYDAY OF OUR Lives
wanna find you there, wanna hold on tight
Gotta run while we're young
And keep the faith
EVERYDAY from right now
Gonna use our voices and scream out loud
Take my hand, together we will celebrate
oh, everyday

Gabriella: They say you should follow
TROY: And chase Down what you Dream
Gabriella: But if you get Lost and Lose yourself
TROY: What Does it Really mean
Gabriella: oh, no matter where we're going
TROY: oh yeah, It starts from where we are

TROY and Gabriella: There's more to Life when we Listen to my heart
And because of you I've got the strength to start

Chorus

TROY: we're taking it back
we're Doing it here together

Gabriella: It's better Like that
And stronger now than ever

TROY: we're not gonna Lose

TROY and Gabriella: 'Cause we get to choose
That's how it's gonna be
Everyday of our Lives
wanna find you there,
wanna hold on tight
Gotta Run while we're young
And keep the faith,
keep the faith

Chorus

TROY, Gabriella and Chorus: Everyday (17x)

So Troy **DID** get to sing with Gabriella and all of the Wildcats performed. Even Sharpay joined in, we just pulled her up on stage. Ryan's plan worked!

The audience is impressed Mr. Fulton is too. "Just fabulous! Fabulous! Well. I have one last task to perform this evening." He walks towards Sharpay. "The star Dazzle for this year goes to, of course, our one and only ..."

"My brother, Ryan Evans!" Sharpay recognizes the real star. Our Wildcat Director really did deserve to win the prize.

And now it's time to party! Because this summer is our summer!

"What team?"

"Wildcats!"

"Come on!"

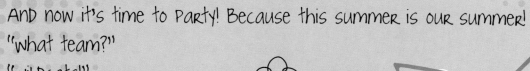

HSM Presents Dance along

Do you wish you could look as cool

on the dance floor as

Sharpay and **RYAN**?

Well, get ready to learn to dance

like a true **WILDCAT**!

These pages are bursting with

top tips and great moves to get

you dancing like a pro.

What *time* is it?
Dance Moves

Dance along to your High School Musical CD as you learn the moves to this hit song!

⭐ Stand with your body in the shape of an X — feet spread wide and arms outstretched at your side. Shout "what time is it?"

⭐ Jump up and clap your legs and hands together, pointing high to 12 o'clock.

⭐ Keep your right hand up high. Snap your left arm down in a clockwise direction towards 2 o'clock and then 4 o'clock.

⭐ Snap your arm back up to 12 o'clock.

⭐ Then squat down and put your hands on your bent knees.

⭐ Shoot your arms, and pump them high into the air left, then right.

⭐ Swing your arms into a 'goal post' position. Bring your right leg up as you close and open the 'goal post'.

⭐ Finally, face your audience and punch both arms forward at the same time as your left knee.

Warm Up Tip:

Leave yourself enough time before your High School Musical dance session to warm up properly! Muscles can be cold and tight and injured easily if you're not careful.

Warm Up Tip:

Ideas for stretching include: Rolling your head around to loosen up neck joints, rolling shoulders in a backward and forward rotation as well as pushing them down and back.

Warm Up Tip:

Ideas for stretching include: Circling your ankles in and outwards so you don't twist them, moving legs from the hip joint forward and back to loosen up. Smile, warming up is fun!

All for *one*
Dance Moves

These simple Dance moves will help you learn to Dance like a High School Musical star — just follow these easy steps:

⭐ Start the Dance with your feet apart and arms by your side.

⭐ Sing the first word of the song, 'ALL', and bring your legs together. Spread your arms out so that you look like the letter T.

⭐ On 'FOR', jump down and bend your knees. Clasp your hands behind your back.

⭐ On 'one', throw your right arm up high into the air and point your finger to the sky!

⭐ Bring your raised hand into a fist and pull it in towards you. Chug forwards three times, each time pumping your arm down.

⭐ Roll your arms, like a boxer, above your face and step to the right as you're rolling.

⭐ Step left and bring your right leg in. Swing your arms down left and clap. Repeat once.

⭐ On 'ROCK 'n' ROLL', bust out your best air guitar moves!

Dance Tip:

If you're choreographing your own dance moves and get stuck for ideas, try keeping a dance scrapbook. Write down ideas that you've had, music that you like to dance to, costume designs and anything else that inspires you.

Dance Tip:

Ask a friend to record you dancing, this way you can watch the recording back and get a better idea of what you need to do to improve.

Dance Tip:

Find a mentor, someone that you admire for their dance skills, like a teacher or another dancer from your class. Ask them to watch your dance-work while you're making it and make the most of their advice.

Keep *Dancing*

Just like Ryan, you now have the dazzling dance moves to wow an audience and bump any competition away! But keeping focused and practicing often can sometimes be tough. Here are some top tips to keep you dancing:

Dance is a great way to keep fit and it's fun too! Find a dance style that's right for you and you won't even notice that you're exercising!

Join an after school dance club or local dance school. Practicing with others is fun and will keep you motivated. You can also learn so much from dancing with others – just look at how much Ryan learnt from Chad!

Get a group of like-minded friends together and form your own dance group. Take it in turns to choreograph dances and teach them to one another. Practice at home, in your gardens, your school playground or anywhere you can think of.

If you've got the passion to *dance* then get *moving*...